A FIRST LOOK AT AMERICA'S PRESIDENTS

ANDREW JACKSON

The 7th President

by Josh Gregory

Consultant: Meena Bose
Director, Peter S. Kalikow Center for the Study of the American Presidency
Peter S. Kalikow Chair in Presidential Studies
Professor, Political Science
Hofstra University
Hempstead, New York

BEARPORT
PUBLISHING

New York, New York

Credits

Cover, © Alliance Images/Alamy; 4, Courtesy of the Library of Congress/Wikimedia Commons; 5, © Alliance Images/Alamy; 7, © Ivy Close Images/Alamy; 8, Courtesy of the Library of Congress; 9, © North Wind Picture Archives/Alamy; 10, © North Wind Picture Archives/Alamy; 11, Courtesy of the Library of Congress; 12–13, Courtesy of the Library of Congress; 14, © North Wind Picture Archives/Alamy; 15T, © North Wind Picture Archives/Alamy; 15B, Courtesy of the Library of Congress; 16, © World History Archive/Alamy; 17, © North Wind Picture Archives/Alamy; 18, © KennStilger47/Shutterstock.com; 19T, Courtesy of the Library of Congress; 19B, © lendy16/Shutterstock.com; 20, © North Wind Picture Archives/Alamy; 21TL, Courtesy of the Library of Congress; 21TR, © North Wind Picture Archives/Alamy; 21B, © North Wind Picture Archives/Alamy; 22, © gary718/Shutterstock.com; 23B, © North Wind Picture Archives/Alamy.

Publisher: Kenn Goin
Editor: Jessica Rudolph
Creative Director: Spencer Brinker
Design: The Design Lab
Photo Researcher: Jennifer Zeiger

Special thanks to fifth-grader Lucy Barr and second-grader Brian Barr for their help in reviewing this book.

Library of Congress Cataloging-in-Publication Data

Gregory, Josh.
  Andrew Jackson: the 7th President / by Josh Gregory.
      pages cm.—(A first look at America's Presidents)
  Includes bibliographical references and index.
  Audience: Ages 5–8.
  ISBN 978-1-62724-556-2 (library binding) – ISBN 1-62724-556-1 (library binding)
  1. Jackson, Andrew, 1767–1845—Juvenile literature. 2. Presidents—United States—Biography—Juvenile literature.
  I. Title. II. Title: Andrew Jackson, the seventh President.
  E382.G74 2015
  973.5'6092—dc23
  [B]
                                    2014034602

For more information, write to Bearport Publishing Company, Inc., 45 West 21st Street, Suite 3B,
New York, New York 10010. Printed in the United States of America.

10 9 8 7 6 5 4 3 2 1

CONTENTS

A Soldier in the White House

Andrew Jackson did anything he could to help his country. As a boy, he helped American soldiers who fought for freedom. When he grew up, Jackson became a great **military** leader. Then he became a great president.

Jackson

Jackson helped win an important battle in New Orleans, Louisiana, in 1815.

Andrew Jackson was the seventh president. He served from 1829 to 1837.

A Rough Start

Andrew Jackson was born in 1767. He lived on the border between North and South Carolina. Andrew's father died before he was born. The Jacksons were very poor. Andrew worked hard on his family's farm.

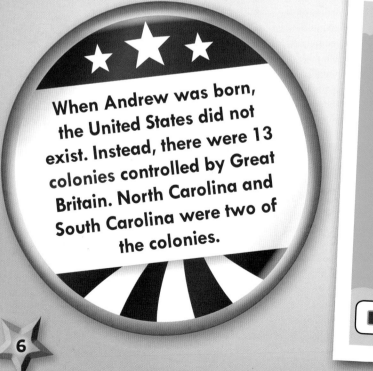

When Andrew was born, the United States did not exist. Instead, there were 13 colonies controlled by Great Britain. North Carolina and South Carolina were two of the colonies.

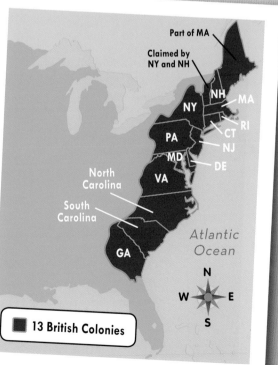

Part of MA

Claimed by NY and NH

NH

MA

NY

RI

CT

PA

NJ

MD

DE

North Carolina

VA

South Carolina

Atlantic Ocean

GA

N

W   E

S

13 British Colonies

Andrew's family lived in a cabin like this one.

7

Young Soldier

Many Americans wanted to end British rule. In 1775, the colonies went to war against Britain. Young Andrew Jackson wanted to help. At age 13, he joined the military. Andrew delivered messages for American troops.

During the war, Andrew was captured by the British. Once, he refused to clean a British officer's boots. The officer slashed Andrew's face with a sword.

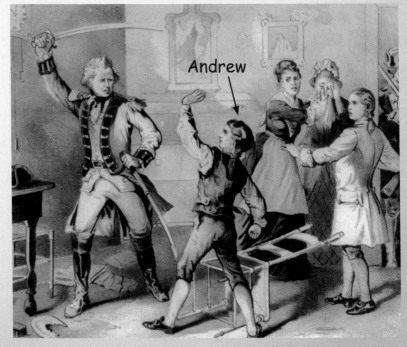

Andrew

The war between the Americans and the British is called the Revolutionary War.

The Americans won the Revolutionary War. Afterward, they formed the United States of America.

A Natural Leader

After the war, Jackson moved to Tennessee. He started working in government. The people of the state voted him into the U.S. **Congress.** Jackson also joined the Tennessee state military.

Jackson in his military uniform.

In the 1790s, more states became part of the nation. In 1796, Jackson worked to help Tennessee become a state.

Jackson bought land in Tennessee to live on and farm. He called his home the Hermitage.

Back into Battle

In 1812, the United States went to war against Britain again. The two countries fought over land. Jackson led troops in a battle in Louisiana. The Americans fought bravely and won.

The War of 1812 lasted until 1815.

Jackson

Running for President

Jackson's success in the war made him famous. To many people, he was a hero. This helped him win when he ran for president in 1828.

Jackson giving a speech to a crowd after becoming president

Many people celebrated at the White House the day Jackson became president.

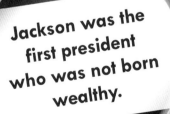

Jackson was the first president who was not born wealthy.

15

Helping the People

Jackson thought some leaders did too much to help rich people. He believed people without much money should have a say in government, too. For example, only people who owned land could vote at the time. Jackson worked to change this.

While Jackson was president, the country grew from 24 states to 26.

Jackson ran for president again in 1832 and won.

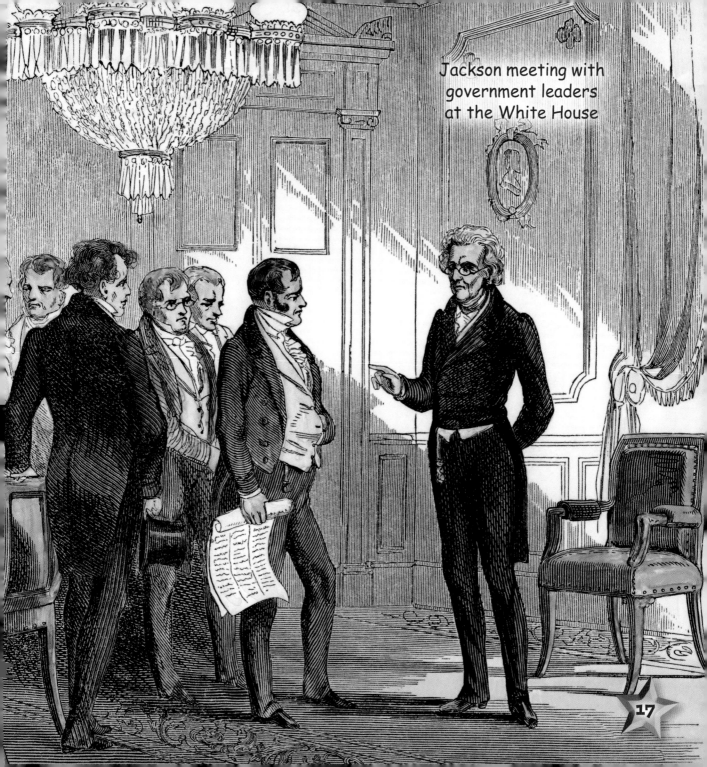

Jackson meeting with government leaders at the White House

17

Remembering Jackson

Jackson showed that anyone could be president. A person did not have to be born rich. Today, we remember him in different ways. Many people visit his home in Tennessee.

Jackson's home, the Hermitage, today

A famous statue of Jackson is in Washington, D.C. This city is the nation's capital.

Jackson's face appears on the 20-dollar bill.

TIMELINE

Here are some major events from Andrew Jackson's life.

1767
Jackson is born along the border of North Carolina and South Carolina.

1780
Jackson joins the American military and delivers messages for troops.

1796
Jackson becomes the first person from Tennessee to be voted into the U.S. Congress.

 1770

 1780

1790

1800

1775
The Revolutionary War begins.

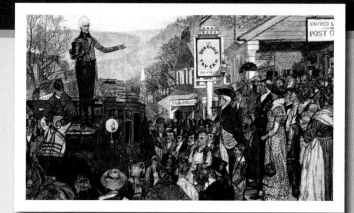

1812–1815
Jackson fights in
the War of 1812.

1828
Jackson is elected president.

1810　　　　**1820**　　　　**1830**　　　　**1840**

1832
Jackson is
re-elected
president.

1845
Jackson dies
at his home
in Tennessee.

"The rich and powerful too often bend the acts of government to their selfish purposes."

Jackson's nickname was Old Hickory. Hickory is a kind of tree known for being strong and tough.

"Any man worth his salt will stick up for what he believes right, but it takes a slightly better man to acknowledge . . . that he is in error."

Jackson fought and was injured in many duels. A duel is a fight between two people using weapons.

22

Part of MA

Claimed by NY and NH

NH MA
NY RI
CT
PA NJ
MD DE
VA
NC Atlantic Ocean
SC
GA

N W E S

■ 13 British Colonies

capital (KAP-uh-tuhl) the city where a country's government is located

colonies (KOL-uh-neez) areas that have been settled by people from another country and are ruled by that country

Congress (KONG-griss) the branch of the U.S. government that makes laws

military (MIL-uh-*ter*-ee) having to do with armed forces or war

23

Index

Read More

Hunsicker, Jennifer. *Young Andrew Jackson in the Carolinas: A Revolutionary Boy.* Charleston, SC: The History Press (2014).

Rausch, Monica. *Andrew Jackson (Great Americans).* Milwaukee, WI: Weekly Reader Early Learning Library (2007).

Learn More Online

To learn more about Andrew Jackson, visit
www.bearportpublishing.com/AmericasPresidents

About the Author:
Josh Gregory writes
and edits books
for kids. He lives in
Chicago, Illinois.